SPOTLIGHT ON NATURE
SEA TURTLE

MELISSA GISH

CREATIVE EDUCATION · CREATIVE PAPERBACKS

Published by Creative Education and Creative Paperbacks
P.O. Box 227, Mankato, Minnesota 56002
Creative Education and Creative Paperbacks are imprints
of The Creative Company
www.thecreativecompany.us

Design and production
by Chelsey Luther
Art direction by Rita Marshall
Printed in the United States of America

Photographs by Alamy (Avalon/Photoshot License, Cherie Bridges, Peter
Carey, David Fleetham, Prayuth Gerabun, imageBROKER, Paulo Oliveira,
RooM the Agency, Masa Ushioda, WaterFrame), Corbis (Tim Davis, Frans
Lanting, Monica & Michael Sweet/Design Pics, Ocean), Dreamstime (Chris-
topher Elwell), Getty Images (Rene van Bakel/ASAblanca), iStockphoto
(EAGiven, LoveTheWind, paulprescott72, richcarey, slavadubrovin), Minden
Pictures (Tui De Roy, Pascal Kobeh/NPL, Luiz Claudio Marigo/NPL, Alex
Mustard/NPL), Shutterstock (Muzairi Mustapa)

Library of Congress Cataloging-in-Publication Data
Names: Gish, Melissa, author.
Title: Sea turtle / Melissa Gish.
Series: Spotlight on nature.
Includes index.
Summary: A detailed chronology of developmental milestones drives this life
study of sea turtles, including their habitats, physical features, and conserva-
tion measures taken to protect these aquatic reptiles.
Identifiers: LCCN 2018043957 / ISBN 978-1-64026-185-3 (hardcover) /
ISBN 978-1-62832-748-9 (pbk) / ISBN 978-1-64000-303-3 (eBook)
Subjects: LCSH: Sea turtles—Juvenile literature.
Classification: LCC QL666.C536 G5257 2019 / DDC 597.92/8—dc23

First Edition HC 9 8 7 6 5 4 3 2 1
First Edition PBK 9 8 7 6 5 4 3 2 1

CONTENTS

HAWKSBILL SEA TURTLES
of Sikopo

Sikopo is part of the Solomon Islands in Melanesia. This tiny island has no human inhabitants. Rare orchids grow in its swampy forests. Yellow-bellied sunbirds sing. Striking green-and-black Meek's graphium butterflies swirl around fruit blossoms. Solomon Island palm frogs call to one another. Near the sandy beaches, red-footed boobies and black noddies perched on shrubs scout the area as they prepare to nest.

Close to shore, in the dazzlingly blue waters surrounding the island, dugongs graze on seagrass. Crabs skitter along the soft seabed. In deeper water, corals and sponges form reefs where thousands of animals thrive. It is mid-June. The water is warm. As the sun meets the horizon, a full moon begins to rise. Buried under the sand for 2 months, more than 150 hawksbill sea turtle eggs have been developing. Now the time has come for the eggs to hatch.

Boys or girls?

Nest temperature determines the gender of hatchlings. Exact temperatures vary by type, but on average, temperatures above 87 °F (30.6 °C) produce females, and temperatures below 82 °F (27.8 °C) produce males.

CHAPTER ONE

LIFE BEGINS

Sea turtles are aquatic reptiles. They live in the sea but breathe air. Like all reptiles, sea turtles lack the ability to make their own body heat. To warm themselves, sea turtles swim near the water's surface to absorb the sun's heat. When they need to cool off, they dive under the waves to cooler water. Sea turtles propel themselves through their environment by paddling their four flippers. Their bodies are protected by armor. The top covering is called the carapace. The bottom is called the plastron. These two pieces are held together by bones called bridges.

SIKOPO HAWKSBILL SEA TURTLE MILESTONES

DAY 1

- Hatches from egg
- Begins absorbing egg yolk
- Weight: 0.8 ounce (22.7 g)
- Length (beak to tail): 1.8 inches (4.6 cm)

carapace

flipper

beak

plastron

Welcome to the World

On the sandy shore of Sikopo, crabs emerge from their burrows and scramble across the beach. Night has fallen, and a full moon hangs in the sky. A mound of dry sand stirs. Dozens of tiny brown hatchlings bubble up from beneath the sand. Their vision is weak, but they see the round, white moon reflecting on the ocean's surface. Crabs skitter toward the sea turtle hatchlings, claws snapping eagerly. Flipper-running with all her strength, one little hatchling races ahead of her siblings toward the moonlight.

There are seven sea turtle species. Each species has a distinct color and shape. The leatherback sea turtle is the largest. Its long front flippers can span nearly nine feet (2.7 m). It can grow to 7 feet (2.1 m) long and weigh up to 2,000 pounds (907 kg). Its black carapace is made of rubbery skin reinforced by thousands of small, bony plates. Other sea turtles' shells are made up of about 50 bony plates. The smallest sea turtles are the olive ridley and the Kemp's ridley. They grow to no more than 100 pounds (45.4 kg). Their shells are typically less than 30 inches (76.2 cm) long.

DAY 3

- Digs out of nest with siblings
- Dashes to the sea
- Carried away on ocean currents

As adults, sea turtles roam the open oceans alone. When the time comes to mate, they migrate back to the waters around the beaches where they hatched. Gathered offshore, the sea turtles mate. After a few weeks, males swim back out to sea. Females go ashore at night. They dig holes in the sand and lay a clutch of about 65 to 100 eggs (or more) that look like Ping-Pong balls. Then they cover the eggs and return to the sea. They may do this up to seven times in a breeding season. Then they, too, return to sea. The baby sea turtles, called hatchlings, will never know their parents.

CLOSE-UP
Zooplankton

Zooplankton are tiny, spineless creatures that drift in the ocean. Baby shrimp, krill, crabs, fish, and copepods are some of the zooplankton that sea turtle hatchlings eat.

FEATURED FAMILY

First Meal

The female hatchling's brain senses Earth's magnetic field. It directs her to furiously paddle her flippers until she reaches the South Pacific Ocean. Here she is picked up by the South Equatorial Current. This swiftly moving stream of water carries the hatchling hundreds of miles out to sea. She encounters a dense carpet of slowly swirling, floating seaweed. Safely hiding under the green canopy, she pokes her nose up for a quick breath every few minutes. A tiny shrimp clings to the seaweed. The hatchling snatches the creature with her beak and swallows her first meal.

Sea turtles lay a clutch of about
65 TO 100 EGGS.

1 YEAR

- ▸ Can hold breath for several minutes
- ▸ Floats in seaweed mat
- ▸ Weight: 1.6 pounds (0.7 kg)
- ▸ Shell length: 3.5 inches (8.9 cm)

CLOSE-UP
Beak

Sea turtles do not have teeth. To eat,
they use their hard, sharp beak to slice
off mouthfuls of food or to crush
the shells of prey. Beaks are made of
keratin—the same substance found in
human fingernails.

CHAPTER TWO

EARLY ADVENTURES

A sea turtle's life is filled with danger. On land and near shore, sea-birds and crabs race to grab hatchlings. Around reefs and in shallow water, sharks and other large fish may devour young sea turtles. The safest place for hatchlings is far out at sea where the ocean is mostly devoid of large predators. Too weak to swim for very long, hatchlings ride currents that move in circles around the open ocean. Sea turtles depend on sunshine and warmth to digest their food and grow. Floating mats of seaweed that also get caught up in ocean currents provide the perfect habitat for growing sea turtles. The beaches where sea turtles hatch and the currents they ride vary by species.

② YEARS

- ► Flippers grow stronger
- ► Chases shrimp underneath the seaweed mat

④ YEARS

- ► Swims away from mat but always returns
- ► Strengthens muscles
- ► Weight: 14 pounds (6.4 kg)
- ► Shell length: 9.5 inches (24.1 cm)

During the first 10 years of life, sea turtles may grow to more than 70 times their hatching weight. Juveniles remain close by their floating seaweed mats. Algae and zooplankton are abundant, and the mobile habitat provides some protection. After several years, sea turtles return to the open sea to hunt and forage. Sea turtles have a highly developed sense of smell because of a special area on the roof of the mouth called the Jacobson's organ. This organ detects the chemical signals of small fish, crustaceans, jellies, worms, algae—whatever organisms can be eaten.

CLOSE-UP
Holding their breath

While swimming, sea turtles hold their breath underwater for four to five minutes. Resting or sleeping sea turtles can stay underwater for six hours. Spongy tissue in the mouth and throat absorbs oxygen from the water.

— FEATURED FAMILY —

Look Who's Exploring

The female hawksbill sea turtle is now four years old. She weighs about 14 pounds (6.4 kg). From beak to tail, she would almost cover a sheet of note-book paper. On this late June morning, the sea is calm, and the sky is sunny. The sea turtle paddles through the water, away from the edge of the seaweed mat. Filling her lungs with air, she floats on the water's surface, soaking up the warm sunshine. The current begins to pull her away from her seaweed mat. She quickly paddles back to the safety of the mat. Despite her curiosity, instinct tells her that she's not yet strong or skilled enough to survive in the open sea.

5 YEARS

▸ Survives a hurricane
▸ Practices diving to strengthen lungs

7 YEARS

▸ Leaves the floating mat for good
▸ Heads for open sea to find a reef habitat
▸ Weight: 30 pounds (13.6 kg)
▸ Shell length: 15 inches (38.1 cm)

CLOSE-UP
Salty tears

Sea turtles' saltwater habitats create a buildup of excess salt in their bodies. Salty fluid seeps out of tiny holes located near the sea turtles' eyes—similar to tears.

FEATURED **FAMILY**

Give It a Try

Another three years have passed. The hawksbill sea turtle's shell is longer than a bowling pin. Her chest and flipper muscles are strong. She swims away from her seaweed mat for the last time. She looks upward and sees nothing but blue sky. She dips her head underwater and sees nothing but blue water. Is she lost? No. Something in her brain tells her exactly which way to go. She sets off paddling east—back toward the coral reefs of the Solomon Islands.

Sea turtles hold their **BREATH** for **4 TO 5 MINUTES.**

8 YEARS

▸ Arrives at Solomon Islands
▸ Takes up residence at Haipi Reef

10 YEARS

▸ Claims a cave in which to hide at night
▸ Feeds on sponges at neighboring reefs
▸ Weight: 56 pounds (25.4 kg)
▸ Shell length: 1.5 feet (0.5 m)

CLOSE-UP
Cleaning station

Animals form partnerships at coral reef cleaning stations. Cleaner fish and shrimp pick dead skin and harmful animals or plants off larger animals' bodies. This helps the animals stay healthy, and the cleaners get a free meal.

CHAPTER THREE

LIFE LESSONS

Sea turtles have varied diets based on their different habitats. Leatherbacks feed mostly on jellyfish that drift on ocean currents. Kemp's and olive ridleys hunt invertebrates in shallow coastal waters. Hawksbills feed primarily on sponges found at coral reefs. Flatback sea turtles hunt soft-bodied animals such as sea cucumbers and squids. Green sea turtles have a completely vegetarian diet. They munch on algae, seaweed, and other plants. Loggerheads forage for clams, mussels, and crabs on the seabed. If necessary, sea turtles can go several months without food, but they may weaken and fall ill.

As they roam the world's oceans, sea turtles follow currents. These fast-flowing streams help sea turtles travel widely without expending a lot of energy. Without currents pushing them along, leatherback sea turtles can swim nearly six miles (9.7 km) per hour. Other sea turtles

20 YEARS

- Full-grown
- Weight: 140 pounds (63.5 kg)
- Shell length: 2.8 feet (0.9 m)

This Is How It's Done

The Sikopo hawksbill sea turtle is back in the Solomon Islands. She arrives at Munda Reef, a popular cleaning station. Sinking below the waves, she comes to rest on an enormous barrel coral. Immediately, a surgeonfish goes to work on the algae that has collected on the sea turtle's carapace. Her shell is sensitive. She can feel every touch of the surgeonfish's mouth. Cleaner wrasses begin nibbling at her neck and flippers. Regular cleaning will help the sea turtle stay healthy.

max out at less than two miles (3.2 km) per hour. Sea turtles cannot outpace predators on land or in the water. Only about 1 in 3,000 hatchlings survives from the nest to adulthood. On land, hatchlings fall prey to seabirds, crabs, raccoons, and other predators. At sea, young sea turtles have myriad enemies, from sharks and groupers to mackerels and barracudas. Adult sea turtles are better protected by their shells but are still no match for orcas and large sharks, such as tiger and great white sharks. Leatherbacks brave the open ocean. Most other sea turtles live along coasts or around coral reefs, where large sharks are less common. Ledges and rock crevices also provide hiding places for sea turtles in these areas.

Sea turtles typically reproduce every three to six years. Different species mature at different ages. Olive and Kemp's ridleys typically nest by age 10. Hawksbills mate at 20 to 25 years old, and loggerheads may be 30 years old. Green sea turtles take a long time to reach maturity—up to 50 years. If sea turtles can survive the many perils of life at sea, they can live to be 50, 70, or even 100 years old.

Swallowing food

A sea turtle's tongue is lined with hundreds of cone-shaped structures called papillae. The papillae grip food and hold it in place, while throat muscles contract to squeeze out water.

(22) **YEARS**

- Mates for the first time
- Lays 4 clutches of 130–160 eggs
- Will nest every three years from now on

Nesting

Once a female begins laying eggs, she ignores everything around her. Most sea turtles take hours to nest, but hawksbills can dig a nest, lay and bury eggs, and return to the sea in about 45 minutes.

──────── FEATURED 🐢 FAMILY ────────

Practice Makes Perfect

The 15-year-old hawksbill finds herself at Roviana Lagoon. She cruises above the colorful reef. She spots an orange thistle-fan sponge growing in a rock crevice. She drifts down and rests her front flippers on the rock. Then she reaches her long, sharp beak into the crevice and slices off a chunk of sponge. Suddenly, a dark shadow passes overhead. A reef shark! The sea turtle sinks. She lies motionless. Her shell is camouflaged among the brown and yellow rocks and corals. The shark swims on, and the sea turtle returns to feeding.

Only about **ONE IN 3,000** hatchlings survives from the nest to adulthood.

(55) **YEARS**

▸ End of life

CHAPTER FOUR

SEA TURTLE SPOTTING

Sea turtle populations have been steadily declining for decades. Scientists are concerned about the future of sea turtles around the world. All seven species are endangered. While it is illegal in most places for people to touch sea turtles and their eggs, the reptiles still face many threats. Rising water temperatures (an effect of climate change) and pollution are making sea turtles sick. One disease causes warty growths on sea turtles' eyes and mouths, making eating difficult. And sea turtles sometimes mistake garbage for food. Many sea turtles drown when they get caught by huge fishing nets or hooks. Construction on beaches destroys vital nesting sites, and lighted buildings can draw hatchlings away from the sea, where they perish in the sand.

The hawksbill is the most endangered sea turtle. For thousands of years, its beautiful shell has been used to make jewelry, combs, and other ornaments. In 1975, these items, known as tortoiseshell, were banned in many countries. But some countries continue to allow the hunting of hawksbills. Only about 25,000 nesting female hawksbills remain on the planet today.

One place where hawksbill and other sea turtles can nest in safety is Dry Tortugas National Park. This protected area is located 67 miles (108 km) west of Key West, Florida. It is one of North America's most active nesting sites. Scientists have been monitoring sea turtle nesting activity at the park since 1980. In certain places, removing some sea turtle eggs from a nest is actually helpful. In Costa Rica, thousands of sea turtles come ashore to nest at the same time. The nests can be overcrowded, and eggs can be damaged. Broken eggs can poison and destroy healthy eggs. For this reason, it is legal to collect eggs within 36 hours of being laid. Many people gather the eggs for food. This leaves a smaller number of eggs, but all have a greater chance of developing properly.

The shift in seasonal temperatures that is occurring on Earth also affects sea turtles. They often find themselves stranded in places that are too cold. The South Carolina Aquarium in Charleston, the Georgia Sea Turtle Center on Jekyll Island, and the Mote Marine Laboratory in Sarasota, Florida, are just some of the places where cold-stunned sea turtles are nursed back to health. As humans continue to expand their use of the oceans, sea turtles will need more of our help to survive.

SNAPSHOTS

Flatback sea turtles are found only around northern Australia, southern Indonesia, and southern Papua New Guinea. They typically stay close to shore, rarely venturing into the open sea.

Depending on their location, **Kemp's ridley sea turtles** eat a variety of foods, from crabs and fish to sea urchins and jellyfish, as well as seaweed and algae.

Loggerhead sea turtles weigh up to 450 pounds (204 kg), with shells about 4 feet (1.2 m) long. They can be found in the Mediterranean Sea and the Atlantic, Pacific, and Indian oceans.

Green sea turtles are widespread in warm subtropical and tropical ocean waters. They nest in more than 80 countries and are about the same size as loggerheads.

In 1995, a record-setting half million **olive ridley sea turtles** came ashore as a group, called an *arribada*, to nest. They laid about 10 million eggs on the shores of Costa Rica.

Leatherback sea turtles are more tolerant of cold water than other sea turtles. They have been spotted as far north as Canada and Norway and as far south as New Zealand.

Hawksbill sea turtles mainly inhabit warm coral reefs in the Atlantic, Indian, and Pacific oceans. Their shells are about 35 inches (88.9 cm) long, and they weigh about 150 pounds (68 kg).

Feeding on jellyfish, sea cucumbers, and other invertebrates, **flatback sea turtles** grow to about 3 feet (0.9 m) long and can weigh up to 200 pounds (90.7 kg).

Olive ridley sea turtles primarily nest on warm Pacific shores of the Americas and along the northeastern coast of South America. They prefer warmer waters than **Kemp's ridleys**.

Leatherback sea turtles can dive to depths of 4,200 feet (1,280 m)—deeper than any other turtle—and can stay down for as long as 85 minutes.

Scientists tracked a **loggerhead sea turtle** that traveled a record-setting 12,774 miles (20,558 km) from Indonesia to Oregon and Hawaii and then back to Indonesia in 674 days.

Kemp's ridley sea turtles mostly inhabit coastal waters and bays of the Gulf of Mexico and the northern Atlantic Ocean.

Green sea turtle hatchlings eat small fish and crustaceans, but as adults they become vegetarians, eating only algae, seagrass, seaweed, and plants.

WORDS to Know

camouflaged   hidden by blending into the shape or color of
the environment

clutch   a group of eggs produced and incubated at the same time

crustaceans   animals with no backbone that have a shell covering a
soft body

endangered   at risk of disappearing from the Earth forever

invertebrates   animals that lack a backbone, including shellfish, insects,
and worms

magnetic field   the poorly understood invisible force surrounding the
Earth that guides the pull or push of a magnet in a
particular direction

migrate   to undertake a seasonal journey from one place to another

species   a group of living beings with shared characteristics and
the ability to reproduce with one another

LEARN MORE

Books

Grunbaum, Mara. *Sea Turtles*. New York: Children's Press, 2018.

Witherington, Blair, and Dawn Witherington. *Our Sea Turtles: A Practical Guide for the Atlantic and Gulf, from Canada to Mexico*. Sarasota, Fla.: Pineapple Press, 2015.

Young, Karen Romano, and Daniel Raven-Ellison. *Mission: Sea Turtle Rescue; All about Sea Turtles and How to Save Them*. Washington, D.C.: National Geographic Kids, 2015.

Websites

"Green Sea Turtle." National Geographic Kids. https://kids.nationalgeographic .com/animals/reptiles/green-sea-turtle/.

"Sea Turtle." WWF. https://www.worldwildlife.org/species/sea-turtle.

"Sea Turtles." Defenders of Wildlife. https://defenders.org/wildlife/sea -turtles.

Documentaries

Greene, Patrick. "Thailand Sea Turtles." *Ocean Mysteries with Jeff Corwin*, season 4, episode 22. Ampersand Media, 2015.

Sea Turtle Rescue, 6 episodes. Smithsonian Earth, 2017.

Stringer, Nick. *Turtle: The Incredible Journey*. Film and Music Entertainment, 2009.

Note: Every effort has been made to ensure that any websites listed above were active at the time of publication. However, because of the nature of the Internet, it is impossible to guarantee that these sites will remain active indefinitely or that their contents will not be altered.

Visit

GEORGIA SEA TURTLE CENTER

Visitors can watch veterinarians work on rescued sea turtles in the hospital and see recuperating turtles.

214 Stable Road
Jekyll Island, GA 31527

SEATTLE AQUARIUM

The Pacific Northwest's leader in sea turtle rescue and rehabilitation.

1483 Alaskan Way
Seattle, WA 98101

THE TURTLE HOSPITAL

Visitors are invited to take a behind-the-scenes tour of the hospital and rehabilitation area.

2396 Overseas Highway
Marathon, FL 33050

VANCOUVER AQUARIUM

The daily Sea Turtle Talk features rescued sea turtles and their stories.

845 Avison Way
Vancouver, BC
Canada V6G 3E2

INDEX